SCANDINAVIAN COUNTRY

SCANDINAVIAN COUNTRY

Pamela Diaconis

FRIEDMAN/FAIRFAX
PUBLISHERS

A FRIEDMAN/FAIRFAX BOOK

© 1999 by Michael Friedman Publishing Group, Inc.

Library of Congress Cataloging-in-Publication Data available upon request.

ISBN 1-56799-721-X

Editor: Reka Simonsen
Art Director: Jeff Batzli
Layout Design: Jennifer Markson
Photography Editor: Wendy Missan
Production Director: Karen Matsu Greenberg

Color separations by Colourscan Overseas Pte Ltd.
Printed in Hong Kong by Midas Printing Limited

1 3 5 7 9 10 8 6 4 2

For bulk purchases and special sales, please contact:
Friedman/Fairfax Publishers
Attention: Sales Department
15 West 26th Street
New York, New York 10010
212/685-6610   FAX 212/685-1307

Visit our website:
http://www.metrobooks.com

To all those kindred spirits on the quest for that elusive perfect home decor item:
May our journey never end.

Contents

INTRODUCTION

When one thinks of Scandinavian style, often the first thing that comes to mind is the very basic "stick" furniture in white or blonde wood arranged in stark white rooms with little or no texture. In actuality, Scandinavian country style is much more complex. Developed slowly over hundreds of years, heirlooms passed down from generation to generation sit alongside newer beautiful, yet functional, items that are constantly being added. Maintaining a respect for the past as well as a fascination with the future, Scandinavian country style is pure dichotomy. It combines the extreme ends of the continuum, from ornately gilded mirrors and elaborately painted walls to bare wooden floors and rustic furniture. The striking result is the ultimate in eclecticism.

In this book, we will journey through the Land of the Midnight Sun. Along the way, a true picture of the Nordic cultures will be revealed through the settings and homes in which they live.

Many factors were involved in creating a unique Scandinavian style. Sweden, Denmark, Finland, Norway, and Iceland are isolated from the rest of the world, which has resulted in the development of a common culture and style unlike any other. This segregation has been both a blessing and a curse for the Scandinavians. They relish their individuality and are extremely nationalistic, but they are not always readily accepted by their European counterparts, which can make commerce difficult. In addition, there have been many wars between the Scandinavians over the centuries. At one point or another, all of these countries have been united under a common ruler, resulting in shared information and experiences. Ties are further strengthened by way of similar languages.

The climate and terrain throughout the Nordic peninsula are quite severe. Half of the entire area of Scandinavia is covered in snow for a full six months of the year, and in Iceland there are still six active volcanoes. Due to the fact that much of Scandinavia lies within the Arctic Circle, it remains dark during most of the winter day for three

OPPOSITE: *Because much of the surface of Scandinavia is covered with water, it is sometimes easier to travel by boat than overland. The Vikings, whose name derived from the word* vika, *meaning a creek leading out to the sea, reached the New World hundreds of years before Columbus.*

ABOVE: *Rough terrain and scarce resources caused many Scandinavians to live far from one another. This led to the custom of entertaining friends at home and having them stay overnight, thus reinforcing the importance of the home in Nordic culture. To welcome visitors, Scandinavians often light the way to their houses with luminaria, as seen here, or ice candles placed directly onto the snow.*

OPPOSITE: *Once the ground is covered with snow, what little daylight there is becomes magnified by the reflection. Here, the sun peeks its head above the horizon and gives a mystical glow to this snow-covered Norwegian forest.*

months—in some areas, the sun doesn't venture above the horizon at all for weeks, and even when it finally does appear, it may only shine for a few minutes before retreating again. Through the centuries, these long, dark days have required the entire family to spend many hours together in the home, so naturally the home is of great importance to the Scandinavian people.

Winter lasts so long that Scandinavians have named its different parts: autumn/winter, which is the most depressing because it reminds them that this is merely the beginning of months of darkness; high winter, which at least offers Christmas to relieve some of the gloominess; and spring/winter, which is the most hopeful, since summer is just around the corner. Of course, these same locations experience twenty-four hours of continuous daylight for weeks in the summer, but somehow nothing can quite make up for the lack of sunshine during the winter. This feast-or-famine approach to daylight results in an obsession with the sun for most Scandinavians. To them, the sun is life itself.

Fortunately, the long days in summer help to make up for the short growing season, although only a small percentage of Nordic land is arable since much of it is rocky, mountainous, or above the Arctic Circle. Water, whether coastal or in the form of lakes and fjords, is prevalent and abundant with marine life, causing the majority of the population to live within a short distance of a good water source. Timber is the most common building material in Scandinavia, although Iceland is an exception since its active volcanoes make it essentially treeless. Most other natural resources are limited.

Scandinavians have had to learn to live in harmony with their inimical environment over the centuries. Out of respect, they have developed a great affinity for preserving it, becoming some of the staunchest proponents of the environmental movement. Some would say that for the Nordic people, nature is their religion. Scandinavians revel in nature's beauty and seek every opportunity to be outside, no matter what the season. Mother Nature provides a respite from city life

ABOVE: *The verdant environment of grass and trees combines with the blue sky and water to create a blanket of color along the Scandinavian countryside. This home, which overlooks Geiranger Fjord in Norway, is so much a part of the landscape that flowers have taken root in its sod roof.*

ABOVE: *Being one with nature is very important for Scandinavians. This Swedish scene is typical of what one might see on a beautiful summer day, although it would not be uncommon for a sun-worshiping Swede to steal a moment— albeit a brief one—in this hammock when the sun shines in winter.*

with many opportunities for recreation, whether swimming in the summer or skiing in the winter. This love of nature has made its way into Nordic decorating schemes as well. The preference is for natural materials, patterns, colors, and styles that enhance instead of mask nature's beauty, such as clear, light stains for wood.

The harsh climate and limited raw materials have also resulted in the Nordic people's ability to live very frugally. A lack of resources has generated an ingenuity and self-sufficiency that would perhaps not have developed without it. The Finns call this quality *sisu*, meaning self-reliance, determination, and a refusal to give up in the face of adversity. With the severe terrain, homes were often isolated, but those people who had the benefit of neighbors in close proximity would join forces as often as possible in order to hold their own against Mother Nature. In lean years, they pooled their resources to help those in need, sowing the seeds for today's socialist society.

Another factor in the development of the Scandinavian style was the fascination with all things European, especially French. Throughout Scandinavia, one can see influences of French, English, German, and Dutch architecture and furnishings. It is not uncommon to hear references such as "Copenhagen is the Paris of the north."

Of all Scandinavians, the Swedes have always been the most enthralled with France. They have attempted to model themselves after the French, adapting French styles of architecture, decor, dress, and cooking to their modest means. French artisans were brought to Stockholm to work on the Royal Palace in the 1730s. In the 1770s and 1780s, King Gustav III traveled extensively and was most impressed with the lavish Rococo castles in France. It was impossible for him to re-create this grand style at home, however, because the Swedish people at that time could not afford projects of this scale. Instead, he trained local craftsmen in the style and they adapted it to their indigenous materials and frugal mind-set. The resulting style, which has since been dubbed Gustavian, was a cleaner, less ornate look that

ABOVE: *One might think that this scene is of a canal in Amsterdam, but in actuality, it is in the Danish-held Faroe Islands. Carrying on the Viking tradition of assimilating customs and styles from other cultures, the Danes incorporated Dutch influences to create many similar settings along the waterways throughout Denmark.*

relied heavily on trompe l'oeil to make wood appear to be a more expensive material, such as marble.

Home decoration had always been the domain of royalty and the upper class in Scandinavia, but in the eighteenth century a middle class began to develop and they, too, became interested in making their homes more than mere shelters from the elements. This heightened desire for home furnishings created increased demand for finer products, such as ceramics and textiles, which were generally imported. In an effort to keep some of the business at home, the Swedish

OPPOSITE: *Although this view of the reflection of Granvinfjord is breathtaking, it clearly illustrates the severity of Norwegian terrain and the limited availability of arable land. This has resulted in a significant number of untouched wilderness regions throughout Scandinavia.*

ABOVE: *The bright yellow of a field of flowering turnips (as seen here), or rapeseed, which is used for the production of canola oil, is a familiar sight in Denmark. It seems to echo the warmth of the sun during the long days of summer.*

government established a manufacturing office to support domestic companies that produced designs similar to those made in France or Italy. In this way, newly adapted European fashions became available to the common people.

Scandinavians continue to look to the rest of the world for inspiration, but they always modify these ideas to their own sensibilities and materials. They have held on to their traditions with more tenacity than many other cultures and have merged aspects of handicraft with mass production. Still embracing the functionalism movement made popular in the 1930s, the Nordic people do not buy products just to look at them. They believe that using items adds to their beauty. Today, a combination of all of these factors has resulted in a large number of well-designed everyday items.

These new items are incorporated into homes boasting many heirlooms or hand-me-downs that have been amassed for several generations. In the past, children would take over their parents' homes and build upon what had already been started. If the furniture was in place, they would focus on wall treatments, tapestries, and accessories to add character and make it their own. In a sense, this approach continues today. The philosophy is that beautiful items, no matter what style, all blend well together.

RIGHT: *In this contemporary Nordic home, the use of natural colors and materials allows the exposed stone walls and wooden beams to coordinate beautifully with modern furnishings. During summer's short respite from the cold, the heavy upholstered armchair is covered with a lightweight slipcover to brighten the house for the season.*

ABOVE: *Even the aristocracy in Scandinavia could not afford to re-create European styles in their residences. At Damsgard, an exquisitely restored eighteenth-century manor home in Bergen, Norway, unfinished wooden floors combine with the ornate wallpaper and Regency-inspired furnishings to evoke the Scandinavian style. A gilded mirror reflects the light from the crystal chandelier to offset the dark elements of the room.*

OPPOSITE: *In the dining room at Damsgard, limited financial resources and the desire to allow in as much light as possible resulted in the use of a simple, translucent window treatment. Although the European upholstery fabric is quite elaborate, the pale putty-colored finish on the furniture frames is purely Scandinavian.*

CHAPTER ONE

LIVING IN THE LANDSCAPE

Regardless of size, location, or ownership, Scandinavian homes reflect love and respect for nature. To ensure that the architecture does not eclipse the environment, they are nearly always made from local materials. In contrast to the widespread use of concrete for modern industrial structures, Nordic residences historically have been constructed of wood, leaving stone for only the grandest of projects.

Some of the finest examples of wooden architecture are the stave churches of Norway, built in the eleventh and twelfth centuries. The supporting frame of spaced posts was embedded directly in the ground and then filled in with additional strips of wood, creating a lovely paneled effect from an extremely practical method of building. Unfortunately, very few of the earliest of these structures still exist today because the wooden supports have rotted in the earth. After the twelfth century, however, Norwegians learned to create a foundation to anchor the supports, thus alleviating the problem of deterioration. These churches were then ornamented with ornate Viking designs, often including dragon motifs.

In Iceland, the elements are so harsh that some residents build their houses essentially underground, with only the gables peeking above the horizon. These turf homes provide relief from the incessant winds. Other Scandinavians utilize sod or thatched roofs, though none but the Icelanders completely embed their homes in the soil.

Nordic homes are painted in the colors of the earth—green, brown, white, or a combination of hues from nature's palette. To harness the brilliance of the elusive sun, some go so far as to coat their homes in bold yellow, formed from a mixture of lime and iron dust. In addition, many structures in Scandinavia are covered in deep red. One version, Falun red, is made from copper oxide from the mines in Falun, Sweden. Apparently the Swedes got the idea when a shepherd

OPPOSITE: *The stone patio of this stately home is festooned with a variety of flowers as well as a number of trees, which provide an enchanting oasis of shade during the long, sun-drenched days of summer.*

found a goat whose coat turned red on one side after it rubbed against the rocks and then was exposed to the air. Not only does the red paint help homes stand out in the snow, but it also serves to preserve the wood quite well. In Norway, seaside homes are traditionally painted white to help fishermen find their way home.

Architecturally, structures are fairly basic unless they are churches or were built for the upper classes. The frugal Scandinavians have always preferred clean lines and simple layouts. Throughout the region, however, influences can be seen from numerous European countries—most notably Germany, Switzerland, the Netherlands, and France. Some styles, like the dragon style created by adding Norwegian dragon motifs to Swiss architecture, were so well adapted that they are considered indigenous.

Embellishments were added to the exteriors of middle-class Swedish homes in the latter part of the eighteenth century. Prior to then, houses were unpainted and equipped with a plank that ran from the ground to the front door, which kept the snow from blocking the entrance. During this period, many homes were painted Falun red, and porches were added to replace the planks. The entryways provided not only shelter from the elements but an opportunity to personalize the facade. In addition, the upwardly mobile added these porches—and sometimes complete second stories—to improve their status. Often these second-floor additions were not even furnished because of a "wealth" tax that was levied only on rooms that were actually utilized.

As the standard of living grew, more and more people started building second homes in the country. Today, the vast majority of Scandinavians own summer houses, where they go whenever possible and always for *Midsommar*—the celebration of the day when the sun stays up for twenty-four hours. Grandeur is unimportant in a summer home; in fact, simplicity is key. The only requirements are a small plot of land on which to garden or picnic, access to the wonders of nature, and a sauna. To reduce the risk of fire, saunas are often separate structures built adjacent to the ubiquitous water source. This allows family members and guests to jump immediately into the cool (often frigid) water after sitting in the sauna.

Gardening is a national pastime. The need for an outdoor space is so ingrained in Scandinavians that several city governments rent plots of land—often including small shacks—on the outskirts of town for those poor unfortunate souls who cannot afford a proper summer home.

Even the cemeteries in Scandinavia are decorated. In the spring and summer, gardening tools are available to tend the planted flowers adorning loved ones' graves. In winter, the Finns light ice candles on their family plots. The province of Dalarna, Sweden, is known for its elaborate wrought-iron grave markers depicting family trees. Individual plaques, engraved with the names of the deceased, hang from each tree of life that stands watch in the cemetery.

OPPOSITE: *To maximize the light from the wide expanse of sky, this Swedish home is situated on a hilltop and employs oversized windows. Dutch influences are obvious here, in both the design of the house and the windmill in the background.*

ABOVE: *No Scandinavian summer home is complete without a sauna. Usually located adjacent to a lake or the sea so that one can refresh oneself in the cool water immediately afterward, the sauna is often housed in a separate structure to avoid risk of fire to the main house. This example is quite elaborate with its spire, complete with belfry.*

ABOVE: *During the long, dark winters, these vivid homes on Mageroya Island in Norway provide brilliant contrast to the blanket of snow, which can last for nearly six months of the year.*

ABOVE: *These homes in Svalbard, Norway, are virtually identical in design, so the inhabitants rely on vibrant colors to help each one stand out from the crowd. The straight lines of the houses are in striking contrast to the rolling foothills in the background.*

OPPOSITE: *These postboxes, blessed with several shades of the Scandinavian countryside, stand like proud floral sentries within the garden approaching this sunny yellow home.*

ABOVE: *This home on the Danish island of Fanø is bold in both color and design. The stark roofline is softened by the thatching, while the bright orange and black hues contrast beautifully with the blue sky and green grass.*

ABOVE: *The dragon style, developed in Norway, combines elements of Swiss design with Viking motifs. Due to the great amount of cultural exchange among Scandinavian countries, styles often found their way to the other nations in the region as well, as with this home built in Sweden.*

OPPOSITE: *Porches were added to many homes in the late eighteenth and early nineteenth centuries to facilitate entering the house when the ground was covered with snow. Wealthier homeowners embellished the porches with a variety of resplendent paints and moldings. This porch even boasts trompe l'oeil marbling around the door.*

ABOVE: *Scandinavians take advantage of every possible space that can be adorned with flowers during the short summer. All too soon, the bleakness of winter will return.*

ABOVE: *Nearly every summer house has an outdoor space that's perfect for dining alfresco. This wooden deck has an added advantage—a perfect view of the blue water and sky that must have inspired the choice of cushion color. Wildflowers from the surrounding area grace the breakfast table.*

ABOVE: *Scandinavians have a very open approach to property ownership. When out for a boat ride along the archipelago, it is not uncommon to row over to a neighboring island with a picnic lunch. As long as one keeps a fair distance away from the landowner's home, one has every right to enjoy his or her acreage.*

OPPOSITE: *The frugal Nordic peoples utilize all of the materials that nature provides—stone, clay, wood, and plant fiber. The dramatic roofline on this exceptional Danish home is emphasized even further by the thatched roof. The use of bold black with white highlights on the front gate and door reinforce the prominence of the gable.*

ABOVE: *This house in Kronborg, Denmark, uses several methods to make the most of the venerable light. In addition to possessing numerous windows and skylights, the home faces the water, thereby benefiting from the reflections. The deep yellow paint further brightens the facade.*

CHAPTER TWO

WINDOWS, WALLS, AND FLOORS

Most walls in Scandinavian homes today are unadorned and in light tones, but in the past it was quite common for walls to be painted with elaborate scenes. This practice—often called rosemaling because in Norway many of the images were based on botanical motifs—began with the churches and was due to the fact that most of the peasants in the seventeenth and eighteenth centuries were illiterate. To teach people the Bible, church walls were adorned with scenes from biblical stories. Picture bibles were also produced and distributed, providing blueprints for these images and resulting in the custom spreading to the masses.

Most of the time, the work was done on canvases that were then hung on the walls. Artists would travel around the countryside and take orders in the summer months, then return home to work on their commissions during the long winter. On the few occasions when the painting was done directly on the wall surface, the artist would become a guest of the homeowners until the project was completed.

Some of the images were inspired by European designs, but most were religious. Other types of traditional wall painting include stenciling and spatter painting. The stencil motifs are generally botanical, although they are often abstract in nature. Spatter painting appears on full walls in more casual rooms like kitchens, but many times it is confined to wainscoting panels. Originally this technique was used to simulate the look of granite.

The practice of painting trompe l'oeil designs on walls was common in the eighteenth century. One of the styles that became popular

OPPOSITE: *The theater at Drottningholm, the summer castle of the Swedish royal family, is a well-preserved example of eighteenth-century Scandinavian decor. The walls are adorned with elaborate floral motifs and the furnishings are in the French style of the day. Signs of Nordic pragmatism, like the peg-boards and the bare floors, are unmistakable, however.*

was an illustration of an elegant curtain design. This was much less costly than making window treatments from the opulent fabrics necessary to create the same effect. Wallpaper also became fashionable around this time as mass production was introduced. The status-oriented nouveaux riches of the period were especially enthralled with the French panoramic-style paper, which featured elaborate landscapes that wrapped around the room.

The peasants of Scandinavia preferred to outfit their homes with tapestries. During celebrations such as weddings, every piece of tapestry in the home was displayed—hung on the walls, placed over tables and benches, and laid on beds. Homeowners would often borrow additional weavings from family or friends to ensure that every inch of the house was enveloped.

Floors were also decorated with woven area rugs in geometric designs. These allowed the wood to peek through. Since timber was the most abundant natural resource, it was the logical material to use for flooring, which had previously been earthen. The wood was either kept in the unfinished "scrubbed" style or stained to enhance its natural beauty—usually in a light color to maximize the reflection of the light. Sometimes the wooden floors were painted with carpet designs, but this was done mostly in upper-class homes.

Traditionally, furniture was either built into or placed along the walls of the home. Peg-boards were attached to walls near the entrance to hold wet clothes and boots. A mother would lie her infant in a small cradle and move around the house as needed by hanging the cradle on hooks in the ceiling. Poles suspended in front of the fireplace held drying clothes or stored crispbread rounds with a hole in the middle through which the dowel passed. Built-in wardrobes stowed clothing and household items. These pieces are still popular today since many Nordic homes do not have closets.

A major change in the layout of homes came in 1767 when ceramic stoves were introduced, replacing the fireplace as the primary source of heat. With the new invention, the entire structure was warm enough in the winter to allow furniture to be dispersed throughout the home. The stoves became decorative pieces in their own right. Some were embellished with designs inspired by European or Chinese motifs, but most were made of basic tiles with small spatter patterns in yellow or green. During the neoclassical movement in the late 1700s, some misguided souls were so entranced by the style that they chose to ignore the fact that taller stoves generated more heat, and installed low ones on which they could then display sculpture.

Stemming from the Viking tradition of keeping the relatively few small windows unadorned with the exception of a possible fringed valance, the philosophy regarding window treatments in Scandinavia is "less is more." Window treatments are characteristically simple, often made of translucent material, such as unlined cotton or linen, to allow as much of the beloved sun to shine through as possible. For privacy, sometimes roller blinds are used, but they are frequently made of a very thin material as well. Many times, however, windows are left completely untrimmed.

OPPOSITE: *Simple botanical prints in colors from nature's palette adorn many window treatments. Often, as in the curtain seen here, patterns are combined to create a homey effect. The diminutive carved wooden horse adds warmth and a purely Scandinavian accent.*

LEFT, TOP: *Unadorned windows furnish additional storage space for kitchen utensils and a small vase of wildflowers collected from the nearby woods. The unimpeded view of the garden outside provides a welcome distraction while preparing meals or washing dishes.*

LEFT, BOTTOM: *In rooms where privacy is not an issue, windows are often left bare to bring in as much light as possible and provide additional opportunities to enjoy the flowers in the window boxes. The miniature taverna chairs and table are mementos of a trip to the Greek islands, a popular vacation spot for the sun-worshiping Scandinavians.*

OPPOSITE: *Stenciling is a very popular way of brightening up the Nordic kitchen. Coordinated—not matching—curtains provide additional color in this cheery Swedish kitchen, which clearly takes its cue from French country style. Scandinavian design is characterized by a sense of balance: even though the red and white enamelware is adorned with a variety of patterns, this corner does not look overdone.*

OPPOSITE: *Windows may be fitted with window treatments, but these are frequently pulled open to increase the sun's impact. Here, the warm light animates the still life on the writing desk, while the windowpanes create compelling shadows that will change throughout the day.*

ABOVE: *This window, dressed with a simple translucent curtain, provides a cozy spot for reading by sunlight. In winter, the ledges in many homes hold pots of flowering geraniums to add a bit of natural color.*

OPPOSITE: *The walls in this Danish home are completely covered with tiles similar to those made in Delft, the Netherlands. This was a popular—and obvious—way for a farmer to demonstrate his wealth. The architectural details are enhanced by the deep, earthy colors.*

ABOVE: *This grandfather clock is built in and, along with the dado and cornice molding, becomes part of the wall itself through the bold use of color. The lovely detailing on the clock's case is emphasized by the strategic use of linen-colored paint. The cabinet provides additional storage space.*

ABOVE: *Rosemaling is the practice of painting walls or furnishings with folk art patterns. This bedroom is adorned with a design of flowers and columns. In typical Nordic fashion, the scrubbed floors allow the natural beauty of the wood to shine, and they require little maintenance.*

OPPOSITE: *The changeover to more efficient ceramic stove heating was slow, since the hearth was still needed for cooking purposes. This one is made of understated green tiles, but the top provides a bit of artistry. The light from the barely trimmed window in this room is enhanced further by the crystal chandelier and the collection of candlesticks on the table.*

OPPOSITE: *Until the advent of the ceramic stove, which heated rooms evenly, furniture was built into or placed along the walls and pulled into the middle of the room when used. After the stoves became popular, there was a notable increase in the demand for furniture for previously uninhabitable spaces, such as these grand halls.*

ABOVE: *Trompe l'oeil painting was used to emulate the elaborate styles popular in France, which were too expensive for the Scandinavians to re-create exactly. Here, the walls have been adorned with an ornate swag curtain motif and the dado with a repeating putto and urn design. Even with the opulent furniture and wall treatment, the floor remains characteristically bare.*

ABOVE: *The walls of this restored* stuga, *or cottage, remain uncovered, revealing the Nordic wooden construction from hundreds of years ago. Dowels suspended from the beams of peasant cottages render a means of hanging the year's supply of crispbread rounds. Sometimes bread was also made when a baby girl was born. It was then saved and eaten on her wedding day, for good luck.*

OPPOSITE: *In typical Nordic fashion, the walls, floor, and ceiling of this room are all wood, but the use of area rugs, interesting furnishings, and a splash of richly hued paint creates a lovely eclectic effect. There is no attempt to match the rugs to each other— the mix adds to the mélange of color and texture.*

OPPOSITE: *Although this foyer contains only one piece of furniture, clever use of color and area rugs—and the perspective of the painting above the elaborately carved settee—gives the illusion that the space is almost full.*

ABOVE: *This room is the epitome of Scandinavian style as it is perceived by the general public. The Swedish country furnishings have been painted white and dressed in handmade striped slipcovers, walls are simply painted, and the translucent window treatments are pulled open to let in the light.*

CHAPTER THREE

CASUAL LIVING

The key factor in the Scandinavian lifestyle is comfort. The Danes go so far as to say that their goal is to create a feeling of *hygge*, or coziness, in their homes. Although the Nordic people love beautiful things, these items must also be functional and easy to handle. Since families spend as much time as possible together, the house should also be child-friendly. Children need to be able to sit or play in all rooms without endangering themselves or the furniture, which reinforces the desire for a simple, unfussy home.

As with all other aspects of life, seasons play a huge role in Scandinavian decor. Changes are made throughout the house according to the time of year, like adding or removing slipcovers from chairs and sofas. In the bedrooms, the duvet, pillows, and curtains are alternated in winter and summer. Cushions, rugs, and tapestries in the other rooms are also adapted to the seasons. While similar in feeling, the fabrics in a room are rarely of identical patterns. The Nordic palette is very much a mix-and-match affair.

During the long winter, home is a refuge from the elements. To create much-desired light and warmth, candles and fireplaces are used extensively. The glow of the flames reflects off the white of linens, walls, and furnishings. Candles are placed in windows to shine on the blanket of snow and welcome visitors.

At the height of the darkness is the celebration of St. Lucia's Day. On the day when the sun doesn't even peek its head out, young girls dress all in white, carry candles, and sing in a procession while younger children, donning pointed hats with stars on them, follow behind. There is a contest each year to see who will be Lucia and get to wear a crown of candles. At home, first thing in the morning, the oldest daughter dresses up and serves coffee and hot rolls to her father.

The dining area of the home is usually equipped with a plain pine table and chairs. At Christmastime, the table is filled with goodies. Guests tend to drop by on a daily basis, so there must always be freshly baked cookies and cakes to be washed down with numerous cups of strong coffee.

In the summer, every opportunity is taken to maximize the amount of time spent in the rejuvenating sunlight. Scandinavians unceasingly swim, hike, forage for berries and mushrooms, and sun themselves. When they return to their homes, they move their dining tables

OPPOSITE: *Foraging in the forests yields a multitude of gems. Here, fresh lingonberries—a Scandinavian specialty—have been collected to be made into jam or perhaps a pie.*

outdoors for alfresco meals. Often these tables are set with fine linens, silver, and crystal mixed with casual china and serving pieces—another testament to the eclectic Nordic philosophy of using beautiful things in various styles together.

On special occasions, like weddings and *Midsommar*, the dining table is used for the smörgåsbord or *kolde borde*—a wide array of festive specialties both hot and cold that includes breads and cheeses, salads, herring prepared in a variety of methods, several potato dishes, roasted meats, a whole poached salmon, and an assortment of dessert items. The food remains stocked throughout the evening as guests make several trips to the table.

Midsommar is a time of great revelry. With the sun never venturing below the horizon, it is a day of immense joy for the Scandinavians. Swedes build a large maypole, decorate it with greens and wildflowers, and dance around it until the copious aquavit runs out. Young girls make wreaths of seven different types of flowers. That night when they go to sleep (if they go to sleep), each places a wreath under her pillow. Legend has it they will dream of their future husbands. Other Nordic countries celebrate by building large bonfires or setting off fireworks to further illuminate the summer sky. In Iceland, it is said that the dew on *Midsommar* night is magical and that rolling around in it can cure a wide variety of ailments.

OPPOSITE: *Candles are not relegated to only the coffee table or dining table. When placed in windows, they become harbingers of welcome for visitors who make the trek through the snow during the long winter.*

ABOVE, LEFT: *Although Scandinavians are no longer homebound in winter, they still spend a lot of family time together at home. Warmed by the antique ceramic stove, children play freely alongside the heirloom sofa in this living room. The large area rug provides the perfect spot for a miniature road rally or reading on a comfortable cushion.*

ABOVE, RIGHT: *Light and shade are the stars of this space. The effect of the simple window treatment is mirrored by the minimalist artwork above the pine chest. The diagonal stripes of sunlight and shadow add to the graphic impact.*

ABOVE: *The most important feature of a summer home is simplicity. It is a means for getting in touch with nature and one's roots—and it cuts the need for housework to a minimum. Reading material and fishing gear are always close at hand to provide endless opportunities for activity, but these wicker chairs with comfortable striped cushions may be the ideal way to enjoy leisure time.*

ABOVE: *On a beautiful summer day, a secluded spot along the side of the house is the perfect place to catch up with an old friend over a cup of coffee. The fact that the chairs are mismatched and the table isn't large enough to fit the pot doesn't matter in the least.*

ABOVE: *Furniture from inside the house is often brought outside during the summer, as all of one's time is spent outdoors. This is especially true of the dining table, since the long days provide sunshine and warmth for even a late dinner. Here, the arbor above creates a particularly romantic setting, but for larger celebrations the extra folding chairs make sure there is room for anyone who stops by.*

ABOVE: *The smörgåsbord table for* Midsommar *is filled with fresh vegetables, fish, and baked goods. Flowers and herbs from the garden add even more colors and aromas to this table, which is dressed with blue and white dishes and a gingham tablecloth to highlight the color of the house itself. The meal is relaxed and casual, with diners returning several times during the evening to graze on the delicious array of foods.*

ABOVE: *The kitchen is the heart of a Scandinavian home, even for the wealthy.*
This antique hearth adds a rustic touch to a room that could be in a modern home.
In actuality, it is in an eighteenth-century manor house. The bold use of color on
the painted ceiling, walls, doors, and furniture invokes a contemporary feeling.

OPPOSITE: *This minimally decorated dining room is warmed up by the bold use of color. The walls are emblazoned with a bright yellow and blue pattern, while traditional plaid roller blinds add a quirky charm that offsets the stark white contemporary style. Slipcovers on the chairs are a simple and inexpensive way to update the decor.*

RIGHT: *Scandinavians adhere to the premise that patterns and colors should be blended, instead of worrying about whether everything "matches." Here, a checked cover and handmade pillows made from fabric remnants give this severe settee a quaint, comfortable feeling.*

LEFT: *Since very little time is spent indoors during the summer, the need for accoutrements is minimal. In this children's room in a summer house, accessorizing is limited to a few favorite toys and pieces of homemade artwork. Extra chairs act as nightstands when they are not required for seating.*

A B O V E : *A bridal chest from 1827 and a handmade tapestry pillow on a rush-seated*

chair are complemented beautifully by the twin framed watercolor paintings.

OPPOSITE: *Typically, Scandinavian bedrooms are not fussy—and this one is no exception. The two single bed frames have been pushed together to create a king-sized bed (relatively unavailable in Scandinavia) that is covered with an easy-care cotton duvet cover and only two coordinating throw pillows. Accessorizing is limited to an assortment of paintings on the lathed wall between the simply dressed windows.*

RIGHT: *Traditional furniture pieces are livened up through the use of interesting fabrics and paint. The large block-printed indigo wall hanging incorporates both floral and animal motifs, while the daybed has been painted and the back upholstered. The wool blanket and accent pillows in an eclectic mix of natural colors add a sense of warmth to this room.*

CHAPTER FOUR

THE HANDICRAFT TRADITION

The long winters and the difficulty of day-to-day life gave the Scandinavian people the impetus—and the necessary time—to create many functional items. Farmers who could not tend to their fields because of the snow and cold would exhibit their artistic side through their handiwork. Those who were especially talented sold the finished products to gain much-needed supplemental income.

While everyone was working, the elders of the family entertained the children by reciting tales from Norse mythology. These stories expressed the belief that the spirits of powerful animals could be harnessed by representing their likenesses on various objects. Not surprisingly, animal motifs are prevalent in Scandinavian craftwork.

Skills and individual family patterns were passed down from generation to generation. When, for example, a pillow cover would wear out, the descendants of the original artist would copy the design as closely as possible, thereby safeguarding the tradition. However, it is not merely via families that these skills and patterns have survived. The Industrial Revolution came to the Nordic countries nearly a century later than to the United States and Europe. This provided an opportunity to learn from the rest of the world's experience. Realizing that industrialization could rob them of their cultural heritage, Scandinavians vowed to protect their ways. In the mid-1800s, handicraft associations were formed to ensure the preservation of these techniques and designs. In addition, these associations provided samples to large manufacturers as models for production. In this way, the crafts tradition developed hand in hand with industry, evolving into the respect for design that exists in the region today.

The entire household partook in handicraft activities. Not only did the family need to produce most of their day-to-day items, but the children had to prepare for their futures. Young girls were required to provide their husbands-to-be with dowries of fine linens and tapestries. The amount a girl could weave before she was betrothed served as testament to her future capability as a wife. Boys spent many hours carving items from wood, including the large storage box that was used in every home for holding extra clothing. This ornately decorated chest, filled with many objects that the boy had carved, was a wedding gift to his bride.

OPPOSITE: *The decorative moldings and landscape painting on the door panel make this wall cabinet unique. Traditional tapestries and furniture are updated by the use of pink—for the walls, the rag rugs, and the weaving on the chair back and seat.*

Weavings created by the girls and women included the ceremonial wall tapestries as well as table and bed linens, many of which were also embroidered. The bedding was especially elaborate, not in design but in quantity. To close off the built-in beds, blue and white striped curtains were hung around them. On the feather mattress itself lay a matching spread of blue and white stripes. White spreads and pillowcases trimmed with fringe, embroidery, or lace peeked out below additional coverlets with brightly colored woven designs.

Even the coffins of the peasants were decorated with tapestries, although not as boldly hued as most. In poorer households, it was the same tapestry that lay on the smörgåsbord table during celebrations. Special towels were also sewn for use by the pallbearers.

The preference for simplicity is set aside in much of the handiwork of the Scandinavian people. One might think that limited raw materials and the difficulty of daily life would have caused the people's creative outlets to yield rather meager results. However, in this aspect of their lives, they seemingly revolted against the barren terrain in which they dwelled. This has been especially true for the Sami people, perhaps better known as Lapps, who still live a nomadic existence herding reindeer in Sweden, Norway, Finland, and Russia. Their handicrafts are quite ornate in contrast to their desolate surroundings. These include tapestries and intricately carved items of wood as well as bone.

Wooden items have been carved throughout Scandinavia, and not just by the Sami. In addition to the wedding gifts that the boys traditionally created, the males were responsible for making most household products. These ranged from storage boxes of all sizes and kinds to small kitchen tools like bowls, spoons, and butter knives, as well as decorative objects like carved animals. Larger furniture pieces were generally purchased from local craftsmen. The Mora clock is one of the most notable designs in Scandinavia. Named for the town in Sweden that produces them, these shapely pieces—sometimes called bride's clocks since they resemble a bride in her wedding gown—are traditionally embellished with botanical motifs either painted on or carved into the casing. In addition to housing the clock, the cabinet provides extra storage space.

Wrought iron is another popular material for both household tools and decorative items. Most notable are multitiered candelabras that brighten the smörgåsbord table on holidays. Handmade candles are another popular way to add light to the home. Candlesticks of wrought iron, carved wood and silver, and ceramics are all common.

One craft that was not generally performed in individual households was basket weaving. Although baskets were used for many tasks, the weaving was usually done by the poor or disabled. The only exceptions were the ornate baskets used to carry food to another home on feast days.

OPPOSITE: *This elaborately painted hearth was never intended to be used as a fireplace. Actually a chimney, it has been decorated to create an illusion of coziness and warmth in the space.*

RIGHT: *The numerous insets of this corner cabinet are emphasized by the interesting use of color. They give the impression of small floral paintings in oddly shaped miniature frames.*

ABOVE: *Although this room is quite sparsely decorated, the use of primary colors on the walls and textiles in this room makes the space seem full. Most of the interest comes from the embroidered tablecloth and striped chair cushions, but the clean designs of the white daybed and chairs are striking as well.*

OPPOSITE: *A settee upholstered in burgundy velvet helps create a unique dining space when paired with a drop-leaf table covered with a hand-dyed cloth. Engaging shadows are created by the sunshine pouring through the large window. Even when the door is closed, additional light enters via the split window at the top.*

ABOVE: *Built-in beds were very common in Scandinavia. Since the entire family usually slept in the same room, curtains were used to provide additional warmth and a bit of privacy for parents. These beds could also be used for storage during the daytime to keep belongings out of sight. The chair is Gustavian—the French influence is clearly evident in the curve of its legs and back.*

RIGHT: *Since heating homes in winter required so much fuel, the family often lived only in the main room, while the other room (if they were wealthy enough to have one) was used primarily for storage. These chests, carved by young men for their wives-to-be, held tapestries, extra clothing, rugs, and household items.*

OPPOSITE: *The antique handmade linens and converted daybed with its ornate carvings make this completely white bedroom a truly romantic space. The heavy ceiling beams and draped lace create the feeling of a canopy bed.*

ABOVE: *Most Scandinavian homes go through a major transformation in summertime—especially in the bedrooms. Heavy quilts and tapestries are removed and rooms are brightened up with lighter linens. Here, lace canopies from the wife's dowry adorn the beautifully painted twin four-poster beds.*

OPPOSITE: *Although this wall cabinet is quite plain, the strategic use of muted red and green on the beveled edges makes it interesting. The colors are repeated in the hand-woven blanket to tie the room together.*

ABOVE: *Some tapestries were brought out only for special occasions, at which time they would be placed on every surface in the home, including the ceiling. A sign of status—the more textiles, the higher one's standing—these tapestries sometimes made the house look more like a tent than a solid structure.*

RIGHT: *A hanging tapestry creates a unique backdrop for a Swedish wrought-iron candelabra. The rooster motif on the top, which is also found on most old churches, is symbolic of light.*

LEFT: *Many Scandinavian men are accomplished woodworkers. In addition to making cutting boards, storage boxes, mixing bowls, and cooking utensils, craftsmen carve animals and other decorative items. Horses, ancient symbols of fertility, are especially popular. Often these are elaborately painted, especially in the Swedish province of Dalarna.*

ABOVE: *A collection of old-fashioned handcrafted tools is displayed on an antique pine table. From left to right: a strainer, an ironing cloth, and an elaborately decorated wooden "iron" with a horse-shaped handle.*

ABOVE: *Simple yet beautiful handicrafts—shaved-wood baskets, wooden utensils, and rustic pottery jugs and bowls—surround this cast-iron wood-burning stove, creating a warm, welcoming kitchen environment.*

CHAPTER FIVE

MIXING OLD AND NEW

Scandinavians combine their love and respect for nature with their frugality and penchant for simplicity to create an eclectic style of home decoration. The color palette is based on shades found in nature. A background of white is interspersed with light woods and highlighted with splashes of yellow, green, red, and blue. Patterns are created using botanical motifs as well as easy-to-produce solids, stripes, and checks.

Furnishings are a mix of new, streamlined pieces and more ornate heirlooms passed down from generation to generation. With their "less is more" philosophy, the Nordic people are able to create a feeling of harmony among pieces from periods throughout history. In fact, individual pieces are often actually highlighted by this treatment. The minimalist style allows each piece to show its true beauty without having to compete with the rest of the items in the room.

To reproduce the Scandinavian country style in your own home, whether you live in a small studio apartment or a mansion, you must merely follow a few basic guidelines.

Keep it simple. Don't overcrowd a room with too many pieces. Try to leave breathing space between the furniture, which also allows traffic to flow unimpeded.

The most important aspect of planning a room is determining how it will suit your needs. If space is a problem, create rooms with more than one function. For example, a kitchen, bedroom, or family room can double as a home office. In addition, you can use furniture items that serve more than one function, like a secretary that hides away clutter but has a shelf that folds down to provide a work space when needed.

Create a space that allows light to flow into—and through—the home. Window treatments should be translucent and simple, not overbearing. Use white on walls, upholstery, and choice accessories to reflect the light. Keep in mind that there are different levels of light. One is general light that illuminates the entire room, such as an overhead lamp. Another type is for just one section of a room—think of a table lamp. Then there is task lighting, which is directed at just the particular area you need to have illuminated, as with a desk lamp.

OPPOSITE: *The white walls and scrubbed floor of this living room create a blank canvas for an explosion of color from the furnishings, artwork, and window treatments. The soft lines of the antique-style furniture pieces are offset by the funky velvet upholstery fabrics. Floor lamps and fresh flowers provide additional brightness to make this room a truly stimulating environment during the dreary days of winter.*

Formality is lovely, but limit its appearance in your house to a minimum. A home is a place for living, not viewing. If you have beautiful things, use them. Just as silver looks warmer as it develops a patina, so does a home that has been lived in and shows some signs of life. This is not to say that it should look worn and threadbare, but rather it should be fresh and clean, yet inviting. For example, adding throw pillows to a sofa makes it more comfortable, but this also helps to preserve the upholstery. Furthermore, it allows you to update the decor of a room simply by changing the accessories.

If you don't want to create a completely Scandinavian country look, you can pick and choose the specific aspects you like the best. You can apply simple wall and floor treatments in a room that has ornate furnishings. Or maybe you like a more elaborate decorating style, but are inspired by the concept of changing accessories with the seasons to refresh your home periodically. Whatever style you create in your home, keep in mind the credo of the Scandinavians: beautiful things go together beautifully.

LEFT: *Function is an important element in any Nordic home. Here, a partial wall provides the perfect spot to place a pine desk for writing the household bills or personal correspondence. The wrought-iron chair sports an unusual back design and is enhanced by the wrought-iron railings and oversized candlestick.*

OPPOSITE: *Even though it is paired with modern artwork, Danish furniture, which is usually perceived as being contemporary in style, looks quite traditional when accessorized with a crystal chandelier, an ornate wall sconce, an Oriental rug, and a brass vase and candlesticks.*

OPPOSITE: *The boundary between inside and out is stretched to its limit in this Swedish home. The use of primary colors along with glass doors and windows creates continuity and draws the eye through the space. The ledge stores a variety of candlesticks for those times when even the multitude of windows cannot illuminate this room.*

ABOVE, LEFT: *A stairway landing doesn't need to be elaborately decorated to create interest. Here, the monochromatic palette and architectural detailing are enhanced by a demilune table with simple but elegant pots and one beautiful spray of orchids.*

ABOVE, RIGHT: *The Gustavian style is evoked by a sofa with blue and white checked cushions in this contemporary room, but the eclectic mix of furniture and the sisal flooring updates the look.*

OPPOSITE: *A massive armoire with exquisite beveled detailing is the focal point of this room. The chairs, upholstered in bright purple, act as accessories. The wooden floor has been kept natural, and the walls and ceiling are painted in neutral hues to reflect the light streaming in through the simple, sheer curtains.*

ABOVE: *While most Scandinavians prefer white walls, bold wall color is characteristic of the Norwegians. Although it is outfitted with simple outdoor-style furniture, this room takes on a dramatic mood thanks to the deep orange paint sponged on the walls and the contrasting blue china cabinet.*

OPPOSITE: *Leave it to the Finns to turn even a woodpile into an architectural accent. The collection of uniquely shaped handmade glass and ceramic pieces creates fascinating shadows on the wall. Primitive cave symbols on the stone leaning against the wall are echoed by the oversized painting on the left.*

ABOVE: *This Danish living room combines a newly reupholstered Empire-style sofa and a coordinating chair with an English butler's table and basic bookcases. Splashes of color in the throw pillows and Oriental rug accentuate the contemporary artwork hung on the walls. The floor lamp provides extra light for reading.*

ABOVE: *Taking advantage of an otherwise useless space under the eaves, the owner of this house has created the feeling of an antique built-in bed with the simple addition of a swagged curtain mounted on the wall in front of the alcove and the use of an heirloom spread on the bed itself.*

ABOVE: *With the removal of the dolls and the stuffed animal, this child's room would be suitable for anyone. Traditional furniture, artwork, and accessories are updated by the strong use of color on the cabinet and the walls.*

OPPOSITE: *This old-fashioned bathroom looks contemporary, thanks to the use of strong color. The wall reflected in the mirror has been painted a muted purple, which is then picked up in the towels and the hanging pendant lamp, while cobalt glass accents add depth to the color scheme.*

ABOVE: *The use of coordinating colors and fabrics enhances this bathroom. To provide additional storage space and softness, the small sink is skirted. The Roman shade on the window can be easily drawn for privacy when bathing. Otherwise, it is kept open to allow the sunshine to pour in.*

ABOVE: *This typical Danish living room combines antique tiled walls with modern furnishings such as the teak coffee table. The white cloth and throw pillows on the sofa reflect the light pouring through the untrimmed window. Minimal accessories include fresh flowers and colorful handmade glass bowls.*

OPPOSITE: *The styles of this daybed and coffee table may be quite different, but the deep aquatic colors create a link between the two looks. If not for the muted natural tones of the walls and floor, this combination might seem contrived. The candelabra, which appears to be hanging in midair, is garnished with branches of fresh greenery.*

PHOTO CREDITS

©Abode: 16-17, 87

©Elizabeth Whiting
Associates: 29 , 30 left; 32,
33, 34, 39, 44, 45, 61, 72,
75, 82

Focus Team: ©Angelo
Tondini: 70

©Lars Hannson: 19, 20, 26

©Kari Haavisto: 18, 47, 48,
59, 73

©image/dennis krukowski:
2, 5, 7, 22, 27, 28, 38
bottom, 41, 42, 43, 49, 50,
51, 55 both, 60, 63, 64, 65,
66, 68, 69, 71, 76, 77 both,
79 left, 80, 83, 84, 86, 88,
89, 90, 91, 92, 93, 94

IMS Bildbyra: ©Kent Bille-
qvist: 57 left; ©Christopher
Dracke: 56; ©Peo Eriksson:
30 right, 58

The Interior Archive:
©Schulenburg: 46;
©Simon Upton: 85 right;
©Jakob Wastberg: 74

©Jesse Walker Associates:
10

Leo de Wys: ©Casimir: 15;
©Fridmar Damm: 31;
©de Wys/D&J Heaton:
12 left

©Mads Mogensen: 12 right,
37, 38 top, 40, 52, 54, 57
right, 62, 78, 79 right, 85
left, 95

Tony Stone Images: ©David
Barnes: 8; ©Pal Her-
mansen: 11, 25; ©John
Lawrence: 14; ©Jean
Pragen: 24; ©Rex Ziak: 13

©Brian Vanden Brink: 23

Special thanks to:
The Norwegian Tourist
   Board
Fredrikstad Kommune
   (Township of Fredrikstad)
The Royal Norwegian
   Ministry of Foreign
   Affairs
The Swedish Information
   Service, New York
The Consulate General of
   Finland, New York
The Royal Danish
   Embassy, U.S.
The Ribe Turistbureau,
   Denmark
The Cidlik Family, Ribe,
   Denmark